DEBRETT'S

NETIQUETTE

DEBRETT'S POCKET BOOKS

DEBRETT'S POCKET BOOKS
NETIQUETTE

Published by Debrett's Limited
18–20 Hill Rise
Richmond
Surrey TW10 6UA

www.debretts.com

Text Liz Wyse

Design Karen Wilks

Editorial Jo Bryant, Liz Wyse

ISBN 9781870520409

Printed and bound by Butler Tanner & Dennis Ltd,
Frome and London

DEBRETT'S

NETIQUETTE

DEBRETT'S POCKET BOOKS

CONTENTS

6 BEFORE MOBILES: *Communication in the bad old days*

8 MOBILE GOLDEN RULES: *Manners on the move*

10 IS THAT YOUR PHONE? *Revealing ringtones*

12 INAPPROPRIATE MOBILES: *When mobiles have no place*

14 MOBILES AT THE TABLE: *Enjoy the conversation!*

16 MOBILES AT WORK: *Stay professional* 18 PHONE FINESSE: *Beyond phone calls...* 20 TEXTING GOLDEN RULES: *Polite texting* 22 ROMANTIC TEXTING: *Enhance your love life* 24 TEXTING FAUX-PAS: *Know when not to text*

26 TEXTSPEAK: *The texter's lexicon* 28 MANNERS ON THE MOVE: *Living in the real world* 30 HEADPHONES: *When unplugging is essential* 32 TECHNO GEEKS: *Don't be a digital bore* 34 BEFORE THE INTERNET: *How ever did we cope?* 36 THE INTERNET: *Online milestones* 38 EMAIL GOLDEN RULES: *Get it right online* 40 EMAIL CORRECT FORM: *How not to cause offence* 42 CHATTERBOX: *Enjoy the conversation* 44 SOCIAL NETWORKING GOLDEN RULES: *Online socialising* 46 A LITTLE BIRD: *Tips for Twitter*

48 TO BLOG OR NOT TO BLOG: *Have your say*

50 TOO MUCH INFORMATION: *Online privacy*

52 CYBERBULLYING: *Online protection* 54 ONLINE ROMANCE: *Alluring profiles* 56 ONLINE DATING: *Romantic possibilities* 58 GENERATION GAME: *Helping older users*

60 LIVING OFFLINE: *Is opting out possible?* 62 A-Z OF NETIQUETTE: *A concise guide* 64 Picture credits

PREFACE

THE DIGITAL REVOLUTION that has flourished in the first years of the 21st century has linked people worldwide, enabling them to communicate instantly and access a vast wealth of information and resources. This newfound ease and spontaneity of communication has challenged many traditional ways of behaviour. While much has been gained, there is also a fear that our digital devices are distracting us to an alarming extent, cutting us off from the real world and the daily face-to-face interactions that are so vital for our well-being.

Debrett's has long been a commentator on manners and etiquette, reinterpreting codes of conduct as society changes. Innovative communication technology has had a major impact on our identity, relationships and family life, and now is the time to outline a new code of behaviour for the digital age.

BEFORE MOBILES

For millennia human ingenuity has been applied
to the challenging task of COMMUNICATING
as fast as possible, whatever the location…

*In World War I, one particularly brave French
pigeon, Le Vaillant, was awarded the Croix de
Guerre when he delivered messages at Verdun,
despite a shattered leg.*

CARRIER PIGEONS can be traced back to biblical times – the first message-bearing pigeon was despatched by Noah. Roman chariot-racers used PIGEONS to send up-to-the-minute racing updates to chariot-owners. Genghis Khan established pigeon staging posts across his vast Asian empire, and the Rothschild fortune burgeoned when a pigeon brought advance notice of the British victory at Waterloo in 1815. In World War I the Germans strapped spy cameras to pigeons' bellies.

In the 18th century a system of SIGNALLING FLAGS evolved as a means of communicating between ships. Initially the flags were coloured with simple designs, and carried straightforward messages, eg 'About to Sail', or 'In Quarantine'.

Eventually these flags developed into the International Code of Signals, first published by the British Board of Trade in 1857. The original publication showed 17,000 signals using 18 flags, and the system was adopted by most sea-faring nations.

The Ancient Greek historian Polybius developed a system of alphabetic SMOKE SIGNALS in c. 150 BC – messages were conveyed using pairs of torches. Chinese soldiers on the Great Wall were able to transmit messages over distances of 450 miles in just a few hours using signalling beacons. North American Indian tribes each developed their own smoke signalling system and language. They typically used fires of damp grass, which caused the smoke to rise.

MOBILE
GOLDEN RULES

☞ Moderate your ringtone and ensure it's appropriate for all situations. ☞ *Decide whether the call is really necessary, especially in public situations.* ☞ Intimate conversations are never appropriate in front of others – try and respect your own, and other people's, privacy. ☞ *Don't use foul language, have full-blown rows, or talk about money, sex or bodily functions in front of witnesses.* ☞ Never use your phone in inappropriate situations, such as quiet zones on trains. ☞ *Your mobile phone is not a megaphone, so don't shout...* ☞ If you lose reception, live with it. Don't shout into a dead device, just ring the other person back as soon as you regain reception. ☞ *People in the flesh deserve more attention than a gadget, so wherever possible turn off your phone in social situations.* ☞ Don't carry on mobile phone calls while transacting other business – in banks, shops, on buses and so on. It is insulting not to give people who are serving you your full attention. ☞ *Don't make calls to people from inappropriate venues; a call from a bathroom is deeply off-putting.* ☞ Switch off your phone, or turn it on to silent, when you are going into meetings, theatres, cinemas and so on. ☞ *If you are awaiting an important call when meeting someone socially, explain that you'll have to take the call, and apologise in advance.* ☞ Do not have a mobile phone conversation in front of your friends. It is the height of bad manners...

The ways in which this INDISPENSABLE LITTLE GADGET *can cause offence* are legion. It is therefore IMPORTANT TO BE AWARE at all times of GOOD MOBILE PHONE ETIQUETTE.

IS THAT YOUR PHONE?

STEREOTYPES

CLASSIC ROCK:
you're middle-aged and trying to recapture your lost youth.

FACTORY SETTING:
you're almost aggressively disinterested in your technology.

TV THEMES:
you need to get out more.

HIP-HOP:
you're a fashion-conscious teenager, obsessed with looking cool.

MOVIE THEMES:
you're a celluloid junkie, who hopes to pick up a smattering of Hollywood glamour.

CLASSICAL MUSIC:
you want to come across as sophisticated and cultured.

RING RING:
you're middle-aged and think retro's stylish.

FARMYARD NOISES:
you want to appear zany and wacky – keep trying…

Your RINGTONE is a public statement about what kind of person you are; other people may find it boring, maddening, eccentric or comic. You should therefore be hyper-aware of the message your phone is broadcasting.

THINK CAREFULLY about what your ringtone says about you: if you're EMBARRASSED by your ringtone in certain situations (trains, the office, when you're visiting your mother) it's almost certainly the wrong choice. Try again.

Monitor the volume of your ringtone; if it BLARES OUT and heads turn it's too loud.

We all admire our phone's POLYPHONIC POTENTIAL, but we have to accept that there are some tunes (full orchestration, dance club decibels) that are just going to sound silly on a tinny handset. Accept the limitations of your phone.

Be careful about changing your ringtone too frequently – you may forget which is yours, and IRRITATE people who see you blithely ignoring the insistent ringing from the depths of your bag.

Remember there's always VIBRATE. It may surprise your companions when you lurch – seemingly unprompted – to answer an invisible, silent phone, but at least they'll be spared the ringtone.

~ There are situations where mobiles really have no place ~

We all agree that MOBILES are very useful devices, but in certain situations they're simply embarrassing. Why not pre-empt humiliation and just switch your mobile off?

IF YOU'RE IN THE **QUIET ZONE** on a train and your mobile rings, your fellow passengers will rightly view any subsequent conversation with resentment. Only take the call if you can countenance disparaging looks and outright requests to desist.

INAPPROPRIATE MOBILES

I'M ON THE TRAIN!

NEW YORK CENTRAL 3350

HAVE A HEART... If you're visiting a sick relative turn off the phone in the hospital ward.

The hushed silence that prevails in an **ART GALLERY** is easily shattered by the persistent ringing of a mobile. Your fellow art-lovers will see you as a terrible philistine, and taking a call will be even more deplored than crass remarks along the lines of "Call that art? I could do that myself!"

"Is this a mobile I see before me?" A zany ringtone in the middle of a **SHAKESPEAREAN SOLILOQUY** will raise the hackles of theatre-lovers everywhere. Despite the best effort of theatres and cinemas to encourage audiences to switch off, it does happen.

Taking a call in the middle of Madame Butterfly's **DYING ARIA** will be seen by many opera-lovers as a capital offence. When a mobile rang at the Metropolitan Opera in New York the hate messages went viral.

A cheerful mobile ringtone in the middle of **A FUNERAL** is the ultimate social *faux-pa*s. No matter how quickly you scrabble for the off button your phone will have shattered the solemnity of the occasion and fellow mourners will be shocked by your lack of respect.

Only take the call if you can withstand withering glares

MOBILES AT THE TABLE

Allow mobiles at the dining table and every mealtime
will turn into a MAD HATTER'S TEA PARTY,
where crossed lines and misunderstandings prevail.

*"When you've once said
a thing, that fixes it,
and you must take the
consequences."*
LEWIS CARROLL

SWITCH YOUR MOBILE OFF and stow it firmly in your pocket or handbag. Even if it's switched to silent, leaving it on the table and glancing longingly at it from time to time is AN INSULT to flesh-and-blood companions. If you're expecting an extremely important call, you should warn your companions and apologise in advance.

If your important call comes in DURING THE MEAL, make your excuses, and leave the table to take it. You can go to another room if you're at home or, if you're in a restaurant, retreat to the lobby or stand outside. TEXTING IS NOT EXEMPT from these rules; it's equally distracting for your companions. Sometimes inveterate texters can be seen surreptitiously tapping their phones, while appearing to participate in the meal and conversation. This tendency should be ruthlessly discouraged.

If the chat turns to QUESTIONS/ARGUMENTS that can easily be resolved by recourse to 3G and Google, don't succumb to the temptation. If things get heated, you can mention that you can find the solution on your mobile and ask your companions if they'd like you to check. Don't reach for your phone automatically.

DON'T MAKE THE MISTAKE of thinking that paying the bill signals the moment to get out your phone, check your messages, listen to your voicemail. Make it a general rule that you don't turn to your mobile until everyone has stood up and left the table.

They're vital communication tools, but in a work
context mobiles can be seen as disruptive, self-
involved and anti the corporate culture. Don't
let your mobile manners impede your career,
remember there's always voicemail and ensure
that your PRIVATE LIFE stays private.

MOBILES AT WORK

You should NEVER take a social call or text during a meeting.

THE CARDINAL RULE is always to switch your phone off before you go into a meeting – remember a mobile on vibrate is still audible during a conversational hiatus. In extreme circumstances, eg if a relation is ill in hospital, explain you're expecting a call. If the phone rings, make your excuses and leave the room.

AT YOUR DESK

Your colleagues will get irritated if they're forced to listen to a series of lurid personal phone calls throughout the day, so minimise the use of your phone. Texting from your desk is not an acceptable alternative – it's less intrusive, but colleagues will soon realise what you're doing. An overt attachment to your phone will make you look like a flighty teenager, rather than a calm, focused professional.

have business numbers entered in their phone book.

WORKING MOBILES

Don't text clients to arrange or cancel meetings, or to explain that you're going to be late – it looks too casual. Use your mobile to make a call, and leave a voicemail if necessary. When using your mobile to call clients or colleagues, always state your name clearly – they may not

Safeguard your company's confidentiality. Don't use your mobile to discuss your company's business in a public place. Chatting on the train about your company's upcoming stock flotation might cause you serious problems – and not just from cantankerous commuters.

17

*"*The single biggest problem with **communication** is the illusion that it has taken place.*"*

George Bernard Shaw

PHONE FINESSE

We all carry mobiles, so our decisions about when we choose to answer our calls are significant. A REPEATED REFUSAL to answer a mobile will soon look like a calculated slight, and a tendency to only communicate by text can appear tight-fisted.

"I CAN'T COME TO THE PHONE RIGHT NOW"
Keep your own voicemail recording succinct; waiting for a convoluted message can be mind-numbingly tedious.

18

Be subtle about **SCREENING CALLS**. If all your calls switch automatically to voicemail, friends may become paranoid about your attitude to their social overtures and assume you're trying to avoid them.

If you **MISS A CALL** and no voicemail is left, try and call back quickly. If you reply with a text, it's a clear indication that you don't want to speak (you can offer myriad excuses – eg you're in a meeting, a cinema, a quiet zone). If you don't reply at all, have your excuses ready ("I haven't looked at my phone all day" etc). We all know that your phone alerts you to missed calls, so it's a calculated step not to acknowledge them.

I'm just going into a tunnel …

If you've initiated a call and then hit a patch of **POOR RECEPTION**, it's up to you to call back as soon as possible. If this is difficult (eg you're going into a meeting), then send a text apologising and promising that you'll make contact again soon.

If you pick up a call when you know that you're in danger of **LOSING RECEPTION** (eg on a train), warn the caller in advance.

If you reach someone's voicemail, try and keep your message brief and to the point. **DON'T GABBLE**, and if you're passing on important information, for example a telephone number, repeat it clearly to pre-empt reception difficulties, or text it later.

TEXTING
GOLDEN RULES

☞ Composing text while you're in a face-to-face conversation with someone is just about as rude as taking a voice call. ☞ *Texts are ideal for conveying a short, instant message. Remember, some important information may need a more lengthy explanation.* ☞ Always respond to texts promptly. ☞ *If you have to cancel an appointment, always make a phone call; apologies will be better received this way.* ☞ Formal handwritten thank you letters should never be replaced by a text. ☞ *Texting is a blunt instrument and innocuous messages may be misinterpreted.* ☞ Use as much conventional grammar, spelling and punctuation as necessary to make yourself clearly understood. ☞ *Keep an eye on the time. If you're up and texting late at night, don't expect recipients who are tucked up in bed to be thrilled by your messages.* ☞ Respect people's privacy and don't text messages that are confidential or potentially embarrassing – you never know who'll be looking at their phones. ☞ *Sign off with your name if you're texting someone who may not have your number in their contacts.* ☞ Don't read text messages when you are out in company and turn your phone to silent when in a business meeting or a quiet zone on a train. ☞ *Don't let the convenience of texting become an excuse for never arriving on time.* ☞ As with ring tones, choose your text alert tone with care – a short bleep will suffice.

"The most
VALUABLE
OF ALL TALENTS
is that of never using
TWO WORDS when
ONE will do."
THOMAS JEFFERSON

Texting is so easy that it's tempting to become a phone lothario, confident and seductive in text-speak, inhibited and INADEQUATE IN REAL LIFE. Just remember your texts have very little nuance and are easily LOST IN TRANSLATION.

ROMANTIC TEXTING

 Emoticons are childish substitutes for words or real gestures. Are you really that desperate or inarticulate? Your love interest will be understandably underwhelmed by your communication skills. :-{

THE TEN COMMANDMENTS OF **TEXTING** ROMANCE

❶ When you've been on a date, and would like to take it further, a quick text to say you had a great time is *de rigueur*.

❷ Don't over-text at the beginning of a relationship – it can make you look anxious and needy, or worse, a text-stalker.

❸ Never send texts during a date unless you've got a lemming-like desire to be unceremoniously dumped.

❹ In the early days, make dating plans and arrangements by phone. Texting is too cursory.

❺ Once a relationship is under way, use texts for flirtatious banter. Save proper conversations for real life.

❻ Never indulge in drunken texts. You might find yourself texting something you regret…

❼ Don't have arguments by text. The subtleties of romantic conflict will be lost, leaving just the bald insults.

❽ Never try to convey romantic feelings by text – it's a crude medium compared to, for example, a Shakespeare sonnet. If you can't rival the bard in just a few characters, stick to face-to-face declarations.

❾ Steamy texting is a feeble substitute for real-life raunchiness. And other people may see your x-rated messages.

❿ Never break up by text – it's the coward's way out.

There are so many ways in which your texting habit can be a source of social EMBARRASSMENT. Why not pre-empt the fall-out by taking some simple precautionary steps?

START OUT BY TAILORING your text message to your recipient. Littering a text to your Granny with emoticons, abbreviations and text-speak is just insulting, while a teenager will be baffled by flowing sentences and perfect punctuation.

TEXTING FAUX-PAS

Use age appropriate language but don't make the mistake of trying too hard to look cool. If you're a middle-aged mum your children will find messages like 'wot u doin 4 lunch?' toe-curling. Think carefully before you text. Much as you love texting for its ease and simplicity, there are occasions in life when a text will be seen as banal, insulting or inconsiderate.

Mis-text *A text message containing information about a third party which is sent to the individual it concerns rather than the person for whom it is intended – a social disaster, to be avoided at all costs.*

OCCASIONS WHEN YOU MUST **NEVER** TEXT

ILLNESS
So sorry to hear about the operation – will visit the hospital soon…
REPLIES
Thanx for the wedding invite – wd love to come.
EXCUSES
Sorry I didn't turn up to yr dinner party – had to work late.
BIG OCCASIONS
Wow! Married 60 yrs – well done!
DRIVING
I'm on the motorway – which exit do I take?

> I'm on the motorway – which exit do I take?

BAD NEWS
Just heard you're getting divorced – bad luck!
MORE BAD NEWS
Hi mum, I've been arrested. Do you know a lawyer?
CONDOLENCES
So sad to hear about your dad. When's the funeral?
THANK YOUS
Thanks for the fab scarf – love it!
BREAK-UPS
This isn't really working – shall we call it a day?
APOLOGIES
Sorry about the red wine I spilt on yr carpet.
CONGRATULATIONS
A baby boy! Well done you…

"y? uz txtN wen u cn uz plain en"
Why use texting when you can use plain English?

Texting evolved in the mid-1990s. By August 2001 over one billion text messages were sent in the UK, and by 2010 this figure had risen to 129 billion text messages. Textspeak evolved as a quick and abbreviated way of communicating by text; it's fine for the *cognoscenti,* but be aware that it will not be universally decoded.

TEXTSPEAK

TEXTSPEAK is a conglomeration of incorrect spelling, acronyms, symbols and no punctuation. The impenetrability (to many adults) of textspeak, and the ease and speed with which it can be deployed, has made it an invaluable communication tool for teenagers.

Teachers are now becoming concerned that **TEXTSPEAK** is sneaking into formal communications, such as exam papers and job applications, and many teenagers can no longer distinguish between textspeak and conventional language. Others argue that textspeak has led to great linguistic creativity and ingenuity.

A TEXTER'S DICTIONARY

ABT2 About to **AFAIC** As far as I'm concerned **AFAIK** As far as I know **AML** All my love **ASL** Age, sex, location? **AYSOS** Are you stupid or something **AYTMTB** And you're telling me this because? **B4** Before **B4N** Bye for now **BBT** Be back tomorrow **BRB** Be right back **BTW** By the way **BW** Best wishes **CID** Consider it done **COS** because **CSL** Can't stop laughing **CYL** See you later **DIKU** Do I know you? **FF** Friends forever **FWIW** For what it's worth **GBH** Great big hug **GISSA** Give us a ... **GL** Good luck **GR8** Great **GTG** Got to go **HAK** Hugs and kisses **IDK** I don't know **ILU** I love you **IMS** I am sorry **IOH** I'm outta here **KEWL** Cool **KISS** Keep it simple stupid **L8R** Later **LOL** Laughs out loud **M8** Mate **MSG** Message **N1** Nice one **NE1** Anyone? **NOYB** None of your business **NUFF** Enough said **OMDB** Over my dead body **OMG** Oh my god **ONNA** Oh no, not again **OTT** Over the top **PAL** Parents are listening **PAW** Parents are watching **PIR** Parents in room **QL** Quit laughing **QT** Cutie **RBTL** Reading between the lines **ROLF** Rolling on the floor laughing **SOHF** Sense of humour failure **STR8** Straight **SYS** See you soon **TBC** To be continued **TGIF** Thank God it's Friday **THX** Thanks **TOM** Tomorrow **TTFN** Ta ta for now **TTG** Time to go **TVM** Thank you very much **WBU** What about you? **WDYMBT?** What do you mean by that? **WTG** Way to go **WYP** What's your problem? **WYWH** Wish you were here **WOT** What **XOXO** Hugs and kisses **ZZZ** Sleeping, bored...

The bad old days when keeping in touch meant finding a PHONE BOX and carrying a phone card or pocketful of coins are long gone. But our ability to communicate on the move has gone to our heads. We need to brush up our mobile manners when we're out and about.

MANNERS ON THE MOVE

I F YOU'RE A COMPULSIVE phone-user you're plugged into a digital universe. But remember there's a real world out there, full of real people, dangers and opportunities. Don't let your mobile turn you into a clueless automaton.

 Are you unable to turn off? Do you obsessivly check for missed calls, and texts? Do you take your phone to the bathroom? You may be suffering from nomophobia, the fear of being without our mobiles.

PAVEMENT PEST

Negotiating a crowded pavement without bumping or jostling your fellow-pedestrians takes finesse, perception and fine judgement. If all your attention is fixed on your mobile, especially if sound is blocked out by headphones, you'll become a walking hazard, both to other people and to yourself. You don't want to mow down an old lady or make a spectacle of yourself by walking into a lamppost or tumbling into a water feature.

MOTORISTS' MENACE

If you're fixated on your mobile and not paying attention at pedestrian crossings and junctions you're putting yourself in danger. If you're mid-text you may well step onto the road without looking and you don't want your survival to be reliant on a motorist's reflexes. Speaking into a hand-held phone or texting while driving is homicidally dangerous and illegal.

CHURLISH CHECKOUTS

If someone is serving you it's rude to continue talking. Pointing imperiously at what you want while you gabble into your phone is the height of bad manners. This is a social transaction requiring eye contact, full attention and 'pleases' and 'thank yous'. Never make a call as you get close to the checkout; if your phone rings let it go to voicemail, or simply explain that you'll call back in five minutes.

HEADPHONES

We're all increasingly plugged in to our
HEADPHONES. But be very aware that
headphones cut you off from the rest of the world
– if you actually want to interact with your fellow
human beings, follow our advice.

*It is estimated that up to 10 million people within
the EU are risking hearing loss because they
regularly listen to music on their headphones at
levels above 89 decibels.*

USE HEADPHONES when you want to withdraw into a **PRIVATE WORLD** and cocoon yourself from your fellow humans. They're very useful when you're working out at the gym, or on a train or bus. They'll even shut you off from the audible mobile phone conversations going on around you.

The minute you are engaged in a **SOCIAL TRANSACTION**, lose the headphones, switch the MP3 player/mobile off, and put it away. This really isn't the time to start multi-tasking, and conducting a conversation with headphones dangling around your neck makes you look like a moody teenager.

When you're involved in everyday transactions (paying in shops, going to the bank etc.), remove both your headphones. If you leave one headphone in and your music still playing, people will rightly feel that this **HALF-HEARTED COMPROMISE** demonstrates you're not treating them with any respect. The fact that it's a mundane transaction does not justify a refusal to engage properly with another human being.

If someone addresses you while you're plugged in to your headphones, remove them and switch the device off, signalling your **WILLINGNESS TO INTERACT**. Don't react with sighs or irritation. People are always more important than gadgets.

Be aware of **VOLUME** and don't blast people with your decibels.

People are becoming
increasingly besotted by their
technology. It is quite usual to
see them GAZING in passionate
contemplation at their pdas,
mesmerised by their mobiles,
lost in their laptops…

TECHNO GEEKS

I F YOU'RE HAVING A LOVE AFFAIR with your technology, keep
it to yourself. Regard it as a private vice, to be indulged in
when you're on your own. Under all circumstances resist the
temptation to sing the praises of your LOVE-OBJECT – boasting
about technical specifications will mark you out as a bore.

"It is appallingly obvious that our
technology has exceeded our humanity."

Albert Einstein

TECH TALK DECODED

You can out-geek the geeks with this useful guide:

☛ **3G** Third generation (3G) is mobile phone technology that allows up to 50 times more data transmitted per minute than with ordinary phones. ☛ **4G** Even faster than 3G. ☛ **A-GPS** (Assisted Global Positioning System) Big brother is watching you, using satellites and phone network base stations. ☛ **ANDROID** A smartphone operating system from Google – it's an all-singing, all-dancing array of apps and widgets... ☛ **APPS** We're all app addicts now. They'll do anything from playing games and monitoring your fitness to forecasting the weather and mapping the stars. ☛ **BLUETOOTH** Short range (10 – 100) metres wireless transmission between Wi-Fi devices. You can talk to your household without leaving your sofa! ☛ **DLNA** (Digital Living Network Alliance) Wireless technology that allows you to play music, and view videos and pictures stored on your smartphone, on your TV or media player. The machines are taking over... ☛ **MICRO SD CARD** With this removable storage device the capacity of your phone to take over your life just keeps growing. ☛ **MP3 PLAYER** You can create a soundtrack to your life when you listen to MP3 encoded tracks on your mobile. ☛ **NFC** (Near-field communication) Wireless technology that allows you to make payments using your mobile. Forget credit cards – they're *so* last year! ☛ **SMARTPHONE** It's like having your own digital butler that can organise your life, send emails, talk to your computer, keep your diary, create to do lists and store data. Just don't lose it! ☛ **WIDGET** A combination of 'window' and 'gadget', it's a shortcut function button on your phone's homescreen. ☛ **WI-FI** Wireless transmission of data and images.

Hermes, the mythical Greek messenger god symbolised the dream of winged communication. But for centuries our ancestors had to endure agonisingly long waits for news of loved ones.

BEFORE THE INTERNET

FOR MANY CENTURIES letters were carried by mounted courier or by mail coach, and the service was excruciatingly slow, unreliable and very expensive. Communicating by post was revolutionised by the introduction of the first adhesive stamp, THE PENNY BLACK, and a uniform penny post in 1840.

First class delivery In Victorian London there were seven collections and deliveries of post daily, and five within a 12-mile radius of the city. A letter sent in the morning would arrive by the afternoon post.

Utilising steam trains, steam ships and underground railways, the Victorian postal system was fast and efficient. **PILLAR BOXES** were invented in the 1850s and by 1880 postmen were delivering mail by bike. By World War I the Post Office handled 5.9 billion items of post a year.

The first commercial electric **TELEGRAPH** system, which used electromagnetism to transmit coded signals over wires, was developed in the 1830s. In 1838 an American inventor named Samuel **MORSE** developed an alphabet that used combinations of long and short sounds, flashes of light or electrical pulses.

Submarine transatlantic telegraph cables were laid in the mid-1860s and in 1870 the Post Office launched its telegraph service. **TELEGRAMS** were delivered direct to the recipients by uniformed messenger boys.

You said you love me stop don't stop

The morse code alphabet had no lower case or question marks, which led to a declamatory, terse style. Telegraph companies charged by the word so most messages were challengingly brief. The word STOP denoted a full stop.

American journalist Robert Benchley sent a celebrated telegram to his editor at the New Yorker, upon arriving in Venice:
"Streets full of water. Please advise."

A vast interlocking web of connections between computers, mobiles and a myriad other devices, the internet is the ultimate communication tool. It is also a massive GLOBAL BULLETIN BOARD and information resource, which can be both overwhelming and indispensable.

THE INTERNET

"A computer terminal is not some clunky old television with a typewriter in front of it. It is an interface where the mind and body can connect with the **Universe** and move bits of it about."

Douglas Adams

INTERNET TIMELINE

1969 First communication between computers at Stanford and UCLA

1970 Creation of ARAPNET network, a network of geographically separated computers that could exchange information via a newly developed protocol

1971 Email was first developed by Ray Tomlinson and @ symbol was used to separate user's name from computer (later domain) name

1973 ARAPNET made its first transatlantic communication with University College, London

1974 It was proposed to link ARAP-like networks into an inter-network

There are over 3 billion email accounts worldwide

1982 The first emoticon :-)

1984 Domain name system invented, making internet addresses more human-friendly

1987 There were nearly 30,000 hosts on the internet

1989 Tim Berners-Lee proposed the worldwide web, based on a global hypertext system

1991 First web page created. First webcam developed

1992 Mosaic browser came online supporting graphics

1995 First commercial transactions on the internet using encryption

1996 Hotmail launched

1998 Google went live

2001 Wikipedia was launched

2004 Facebook was launched, initially for college students

2006 Twitter was launched

EMAIL
GOLDEN RULES

☞ Avoid sarcasm and subtle humour, unless you know that the reader will 'get it'. If in doubt, err towards the polite and formal. ☞ *Delicate communications should be sent by other means, and think carefully before hitting 'send' if your email is written in haste or when emotions are running high.* ☞ Be sparing in your use of smiley faces, kisses etc. Are these symbols really suitable for the recipient? ☞ *Using capital letters looks like shouting and should be avoided. If you want to emphasise something, try underlining or using italics.* ☞ Don't over-punctuate. Emails that are littered with exclamation marks (known as 'bangs') are just exhausting. ☞ *Try not to use shortened 'text language'. Many recipients will find abbreviations irritating or incomprehensible. They may also assume that you're lazy or semi-literate.* ☞ Beware wacky email addresses for formal or business emails. You won't be taken seriously with an email address like 'madwoman@hotmail.co.uk'. ☞ *Don't be a coward and hide behind your emails to say things you wouldn't say in person.* ☞ Your friends may get weary if you overwhelm them with sponsorship forms, links to amusing YouTube videos, chain emails, begging emails etc. ☞ *Bitching about your colleagues by office email is a really bad idea – it's a very leaky medium.* ☞ If you want to make an impact (eg you're sending a thank you note for a present, or a birthday greeting), go for a posted letter or card.

"Electric communication will NEVER be a substitute for THE FACE OF SOMEONE who with their SOUL *encourages another person* to be BRAVE AND TRUE."

CHARLES DICKENS

EMAIL CORRECT FORM

Do you regularly send out mass circulation emails, with no subject lines, an indiscriminately informal 'Hiya' salutation, HUGE ATTACHMENTS and a jaunty sign-off? If the answer is yes, you may need to brush up your email etiquette.

You've been flamed *If you provoke an email attack, you've been flamed. If possible, ignore the flame, or work out what's caused the offence. If you reply in kind, you're entering a 'flame war'.*

ADDRESS AND SUBJECT LINE

☞ Don't hit the 'reply all' automatically. You'll end up sending your emails to lots of irrelevant people.

☞ Use 'CC' discriminately. It's for people who need to be kept in the loop, it's not a catch-all.

☞ Use an eye-catching and meaningful subject line – you don't want recipients to sort through reams of text to find out what your email is about.

☞ Use the 'importance' label sparingly. Otherwise it will be the email equivalent of the boy who cried wolf – ignored because of its frequent misuse.

SALUTATION

Use appropriate language. You'd never write 'Hi there' at the beginning of a business letter so don't do it at the start of a formal email. Retain the same level of formality that you would use in all correspondence (eg Dear Sir, Dear Mr Brown, Dear Bob). If you're approached with informality, then reciprocate in kind.

SIGN OFF

In formal emails you might use 'yours faithfully/sincerely'; in most cases you'll use something more casual ('Best wishes', 'Best', 'Cheers'). At work, add your full name, job title and phone number underneath.

THREADS

Maintain threads (the previous emails on a subject) where appropriate. But if it's a long, complex thread a pithy 'I agree' isn't helpful, so briefly reiterate what you agree with.

ATTACHMENTS

Don't overload your email with system-slowing extras.

~ It's all about having a meaningful conversation ~

Social relationships within chatrooms and web forums are modelled on THE REAL WORLD, and many of the same rules of behaviour apply in cyberspace. The cardinal error is to forget that you're conversing with real people, who will not take kindly to bullying, abuse, or overbearing behaviour.

CHATTERBOX

"A wise man does not **chatter** with one whose mind is sick."

Sophocles

The first chat rooms, called Internet Relay Chat (IRC), were invented by Jarkko Oikarinen in 1988. IRC in turn inspired contemporary instant messaging, web chat and voice chat systems.

HOW TO **PERFECT** YOUR INTERNET PERSONA

☞ DON'T be a **rule-breaker**: read the page for newcomers, check the FAQs, look at recent discussions and pick up group nuances.

☞ DON'T **barge in**: in smaller chatrooms, check that you're welcome to join in.

☞ DON'T forget the **social niceties**: when you enter a chatroom or forum, introduce yourself.

☞ DON'T be a **peeping tom**: participate in the conversation rather than skulking in the background.

☞ DON'T be a **delinquent**: if you disagree with what's being said, offensive or abusive language will soon get you ejected or ignored.

☞ DON'T be an **attention-seeker**: penning your messages in capital letters looks over-emphatic and will lose you friends.

☞ DON'T be a **spammer**: posting ads for products and services will make you very unpopular.

☞ DON'T act like **Jekyll and Hyde**: you might want to reinvent yourself, but your posts will be accessible to friends and family.

☞ DON'T indulge in **digressions**: stay on topic – you've chosen your chatroom for a reason.

☞ DON'T be a **stalker**: if you harass individuals you'll get banned.

☞ DON'T talk **gobbledegook**: your posts should be comprehensible, so try and write grammatically and clearly and keep abbreviations to the minimum.

☞ DON'T be **crass**: it's bad form just to melt away from a chatroom or forum.

SOCIAL NETWORKING
GOLDEN RULES

☞ You don't have to make friends with people you don't know. It's not a competition to see how many friends you can get. ☞ *Think before you tag.* ☞ Think before you poke. ☞ *When requesting someone to be a social friend on Facebook, send a personal message along with the request.* ☞ Always wait 24 hours before accepting or removing someone as a friend. The delay will help you gather your thoughts. ☞ *Don't pester your Facebook friends to join a group, forum, petition, fan page. Asking once is enough.* ☞ Consider your friends' feelings before posting pictures – an 'amusing' picture might have dire consequences. ☞ *Think carefully about your profile picture – don't post glamour, vintage or re-touched photos on Facebook; pouting narcissism will be nakedly obvious.* ☞ Don't post minute-by-minute updates to your relationship status. Out in the real world, relationships are subtle, complex and dynamic; a 'single' update could be a sledgehammer blow to any rapprochment. ☞ *Do some housekeeping on your Facebook Wall. If old friends are posting embarrassing jokes or incriminating pictures, remove them, or even ask friends if they would consider doing so. You don't want your profile to be dogged by the detritus of your past.* ☞ Don't use your personal Facebook account to market yourself, your business, or a commercial product. Create a separate, business-related, account.

"*The* QUESTION *isn't,*
'What do we WANT to
know about PEOPLE?',
it's, 'What do people
WANT to tell about
THEMSELVES?'"

MARK ZUCKERBERG
CO-FOUNDER, FACEBOOK

~ How to change the world in 140 characters ~

Micro-blogging is about disseminating information, news and content as well as airing OPINIONS and OBSERVATIONS. Brush up your Twitterquette and make yourself heard in the Twittersphere.

A LITTLE BIRD...

"Twitter is about **participating** – by which I mean you tweet and read other people's tweets. Then you **understand** it, and get its rhythm. But remember: it is about being authentic. These things are human-shaped."

Stephen Fry

DO

☞ Think before you tweet.

☞ It's a big, bruising world out there and you're bound to get negative feedback. Ignore it.

☞ Take a look at the people following you and follow them back if they look interesting.

☞ Credit other people's tweets and acknowledge their ideas.

☞ Provide information and inside knowledge if you have it.

☞ Be supportive of other tweeters; use #FollowFriday (#FF) to alert your followers to interesting tweeters.

☞ Use hash tags to alert people to topics of interest.

☞ Thank people who retweet you or give you information.

☞ Be punctilious in replying to questions, requests or information.

☞ Retain a sense of decorum. Keep personal chats private.

DON'T

☞ If you've joined the party, then make some contributions.

☞ Forget the anonymous egghead persona, and create a proper profile, with a photograph and information.

☞ Even your nearest and dearest will not appreciate a blow-by-blow account of your everyday life in 140 characters.

☞ Aggressive tweets are rude and will lose you followers.

☞ Over-marketing will make you unpopular. Intersperse promotional tweets with general obvservations and chat.

☞ Celebrity-schmoozing is sad. Being a follower is not the same as being a friend, so forget over-familiarity.

☞ Remember over-tweeting is overwhelming. Your followers will begin to see your tweets as no better than spam.

TO BLOG OR NOT TO BLOG...

The web has turned us all into writers, designers and publishers, and blogging is a wonderful way of communicating with the WIDER WORLD. But beware, there are breaches of etiquette that will give you a very bad reputation in the blogosphere...

Research shows that bloggers spend an average of 10-12 hours weekly on social media sites, with 14% spending at least 21 hours. Bloggers spend another 8 hours weekly reading other blogs.

48

TAKE A DEEP BREATH Think carefully before you post a blog; check the grammar and spelling and make sure that you're confident about uploading it. Blogs that are written in anger, or because you're feeling rejected or ignored, may well be freighted with negative emotions. **ALWAYS ACKNOWLEDGE HELP AND GENEROSITY** If you're using photographs, seek permission and always credit the source. Or if you're using research from another online resource, credit it, preferably with a hyperlink (test it first). **SIGNPOSTING IS IMPORTANT** If you're writing about subjects that you know are covered in detail elsewhere on the internet, then it's really helpful to use hyperlinks to direct your readers to other resources. **REMEMBER, IT'S A CONTINUING CONVERSATION** If someone has posted a compliment, a thank you, a comment or a question on your blog, then acknowledge their contribution and reply. If you're replying to someone else's blog, keep your comments relevant and valuable – just saying 'great blog' isn't particularly constructive. **RECIPROCATE ANY INTEREST SHOWN IN YOU** It's only polite to pay a return visit if visitors to your blog leave links and comments. These are a kind of internet calling card, so you should take up the invitation and go visiting. **RISE ABOVE ATTACKS** If someone attacks you don't take it to heart. Some people are irredeemably negative so don't let their poison get to you. If you feel their comments have value, it's fine to reply, but retain the moral high ground and stay relentlessly polite.

> 77% of internet-users read blogs

49

TOO MUCH INFORMATION

The internet encourages social interaction, but because there is no physical contact it is only too easy to forget that it is a very PUBLIC FORUM, and that anonymity is illusory. You must take positive action to safeguard your online privacy.

"All human beings have three lives: public, private, and secret."
Gabriel García Márquez

IF YOU'RE interested in your ONLINE PRIVACY, adopt the following policies:

☞ **Never underestimate the internet.** It's easy when you're tapping away in the privacy of your own home to forget just how quickly things can go viral.

☞ **Safeguard children** and don't post pictures of your children online unless they're password-protected and you're confident of your privacy settings. Otherwise you might just as well scatter pictures of your kids around the town centre – that's what you're doing in the virtual community. Don't post pictures of other people's kids online without asking their permission first.

☞ **Don't tag unflattering photos of your friends.** You wouldn't want the embarrassing contents of your family photo album to be shown to all and sundry, so respect the fact that everyone has a right to veto.

☞ **Think about consequences.** You might find it amusing to post photos of your friend's drunken antics – they won't find it funny when a potential employer does some snooping and dislikes what they see.

☞ **Use your discretion.** It might be tempting to share the more lurid details of your life – but you may find your children, their friends or your employers are less than impressed by your drunken, vitriolic ramblings about your ex-husband.

☞ **Compartmentalise.** You wouldn't invite your boss or your kids' headmistress round to the family barbecue in real life so why do it online? Adjust your privacy settings to ensure that there are boundaries between your different worlds.

51

The internet is a frighteningly effective way of channelling and disseminating ABUSE, and for many of the perpetrators its anonymity facilitates behaviour that they would NEVER contemplate FACE-TO-FACE.

Cyberstalking *Nearly three quarters of the nearly 5 million victims who contact the National Stalking Helpline each year are stalked through emails and the internet.*

CYBERBULLYING

THE BULLY'S ARMOURY

☞ Sending 'joking' emails that are actually offensive or disturbing

☞ Posting deeply unflattering pictures of his/her target

☞ Spreading gossip and malicious rumours through social networking sites

☞ Disclosing confidential information about the target – eg address, workplace

☞ Bombarding the target with threatening or disturbing emails

CYBERBULLYING can affect all age groups, but is prevalent amongst children aged 11 to 18. If your child seems upset or withdrawn consider the possibility that cyberbullying is taking place.

An abrasive workplace culture can also result in all sorts of e-harrassment, and while some employees might dismiss their antics as 'just fun', their targets might not be so tolerant. If online harassment is a problem report it to your management who are obliged to provide content filtering and spam filtering services.

Safeguard your home email address and only give it to trusted friends and contacts. If you visit chatrooms don't use your real name and don't use a photo of yourself as an avatar.

SAFEGUARDING YOUR CHILD

☞ Stranger danger: encourage your children not to talk with strangers online.

☞ If your child gets an abusive text messages or emails, advise him/her not to reply.

☞ Report abusive phone messages to the mobile service provider; if the bullying is online, report it to your internet service provider.

☞ Although your first reaction to abusive emails etc is to delete them, don't erase. Keep everything as evidence.

☞ Contact the school. The abuse might be transmitted through the school's internet system, in which case they have an obligation to intervene.

☞ If, at any point, the abuse contains obscenity, threats of violence, or any suggestion of sexual harassment or stalking, contact the police immediately.

~ Your online profile will be tested in the real world ~

It's important to remember that creating an alluring
profile and indulging in some TANTALISING
online FLIRTING are just the preludes to romance.
Online dating is all about creating access and
opportunity, but ultimately you will have to take
your cyber-romance into the real world.

Are you looking for a SNAG with a GSOH?
Or perhaps a SPARK in search of a LTR?

ONLINE ROMANCE

ACRONYMS DECODED ☛ **BBW:** Big Beautiful Woman
BHM: Big Handsome Man **BHOF:** Bald Headed Old Fart **BIM:**
Bisexual Male **BIF:** Bisexual Female **DDF:** Drug and Disease
Free **F2F:** Face To Face **GSOH:** Good sense of humour **HWP:**
Height Weight Proportional **IRL:** In Real Life **ISO:** In Search of
LDR: Long Distance Relationship **LTR:** Long Term Relationship
MBA: Married but Available **MOTSS:** Members Of The Same Sex
SITCOMS: Single Income, Two Children, Oppressive Mortgage
SNAG: Sensitive New Age Guy **SORG?:** Straight or Gay?
SPARK: Single Parent Raising Kids **VGL:** Very Good Looking
WLTM: Would Like to Meet

☞ **SELECT YOUR SITE** Choose your dating site with care. If you're acronym-averse, then it's sensible to find a site where you can indulge in more wordy descriptions. Shop around before you take the plunge.

BHM in search of a LTR with a BBW

☞ **CHOOSE YOUR PHOTO** It's foolish to post an out-of-date or glamourised picture of yourself – when you meet in the flesh the look of disappointment will be hard to take.

☞ **READ BETWEEN THE LINES** The online dating universe is riddled with clichés and you'll need to decode them. If someone says that he or she is 'sincere', read 'boring'; 'attractive' is a bland catch-all. People who describe themselves as 'fun-loving' sound desperate, and if you've got a good sense of humour do you really need to say it? Beware of 'outspoken' or 'direct': this may be a code for 'demanding' and 'hyper-critical'.

☞ **TELL THE TRUTH** It's no good saying you love *Anna Karenina* and French art-house films if you're really happiest with the latest chick lit blockbuster and a cheesy rom-com. Even if you feel your tastes let you down, brazen it out – there'll be someone out there who either shares them or likes the fact that you're open and honest. ☞ **BE REALISTIC** Internet dating sites may look like a big box of chocolates waiting to be plundered, but retain a sense of proportion. Take a long, hard look at yourself, and match your aspirations with your age, personality and appearance.

~ The internet will open you up to a world of romantic possibility ~

Once your profile is up online, you'll feel like you've
set out your stall and you're waiting for buyers.
Online dating can feel depressing and pointless
or EXCITING and OPTIMISTIC. You must be
prepared to encounter rejection, but you'll also feel
that your horizons are opening out and that the
world is FULL OF POTENTIAL.

ONLINE DATING

"Dating is **pressure**
and **tension**. What is
a date, really, but a
job interview that
lasts all night?

Jerry Seinfeld

DATING RECOMMENDATIONS

☞ **Protect your identity:** create a separate email address for online romance – you can always close it down if you're subject to abuse or stalking.

☞ **Take your time:** don't panic and leap at the first option. If you're patient a more interesting prospect will eventually appear.

☞ **Make polite excuses:** if you don't like the look of someone, don't just ignore their approaches. Do the same as you would in real life, and say something like 'I'm looking for someone who lives a bit closer' or 'you're not in my age range'.

☞ **Stay positive:** if you're rejected don't plunge into petulance ('I didn't fancy you anyway') or self-loathing. You need a robust ego for the rough and tumble of online dating.

☞ **Try telephone screening:** you'll pick up nuances in a phone conversation that you'll miss online, and you may save yourself time and heartache.

☞ **Stay cautious:** arrange your first meeting in a public place, and make sure someone knows where you are.

☞ **Play the field:** until you're in a 'proper' relationship it's completely acceptable to date several people at the same time – as long as you're open.

☞ **Don't get obsessed:** it's easy to get addicted to checking out new possibilities in your inbox. Remember you have a real life.

☞ **Call it a day:** if you've met the partner of your dreams, you'll discuss removing your online dating profiles. This is a major commitment, and it must be mutual.

~ Sometimes the internet is just too confusing~

A new world is available at the click of a mouse??

GENERATION GAME

Some members of the older generation have chosen
to opt out of the whole ONLINE UNIVERSE.
They feel happy to adhere to their traditional
choices: letters, phone calls, newspapers, television.
If this is a definitive decision, they will undoubtedly
find nagging and prosleytising
about the joys of the internet
exhausting and irritating.

*Nearly 58% of
people over 65 in the
UK have never used
the internet.*

58

IF YOU SPEND every waking moment online and communicate almost exclusively through new media – emails, social networking, skype, texting and so on – you may find it difficult to accept that not everyone is the same.

Don't wax lyrical about the convenience of online shopping and the delights of social networking to someone who has shown no interest in even owning a computer. Respect the decision – make phone calls or send letters (no e-cards!) – and never complain.

If you see tentative signs of interest, then it is worthwhile gently pointing out that the internet has its uses – sharing family photos, downloading podcasts and crosswords, emailing…

WAYS TO HELP

☞ Establish what the person wants to do online and make this a priority.

☞ Help them to choose the right equipment: a desktop pc might be best, as there will be a larger, more legibile screen and a more robust keyboard.

☞ Set the computer to load automatically to frequently used software and sites.

☞ Set up the browser home page with bookmarks to the user's favourite sites. Ensure that the browser typeface is set to a legible font.

☞ Make useful templates in the word processing program.

☞ Go through privacy settings on social networking sites.

☞ Create a reference sheet that lists the most common keyboard commands – open, copy, paste, save.

Many of us feel that life without the internet is IMPOSSIBLE. Perhaps we should recognise that the internet is an ADDICTION and experiment with living, at least mentally, on a desert island that is free of Wi-Fi, mobiles and chatrooms.

LIVING OFFLINE

DON'T BE AN INTERNET BORE

☞ If all your conversation is based on facts/insights you've gleaned from the internet, people will suspect you of not having a life.

☞ It might be easy to communicate online but that doesn't mean you have to do it all the time. Flooding friends with emails, pokes, weblinks etc. will soon become irritating.

☞ Spamming friends with endless demands for signatures, donations and sponsorship will drive them mad.

☞ Boasting about your online shopping triumphs will turn everyone off. Keep your bargains to yourself.

☞ **Enjoy the journey.**
Navigate your way around
town with a real map or ask a
stranger for directions. Allow
yourself plenty of time (no last
minute phone calls explaining
that you're late) and look at the
world around you.

☞ **Revel in the written word.**
Try reading a book, magazine
or newspaper when you're on
a train or on holiday. With no
social networking or online
surfing you might regain your
powers of concentration.

☞ **Indulge in face to face
contact.** The online world
facilitates communication but
keeps contact at a distance.
Meeting in the flesh will allow
chemistry to flourish and
intimacy to blossom.

☞ **Write a letter.** Rediscover
the satisfaction of the written
word – you can experience the
joys of choosing stationery,

writing with a real fountain pen,
and even strolling down to the
post box. And correspondents
will love receiving real mail.

☞ **Do your own research.**
Google hands you the world
on a plate, but sometimes it's
good to look things up in
books, make phone calls, or
ask friends. It's slower, but you
might find it more satisfying.

☞ **Drop out of the internet
rat race.** Remember that the
networking, blogging, tweeting
and chatting can all continue
without you. Sometimes it's
relaxing just to switch off the
information deluge.

☞ **Stop wasting your time.**
The internet is infinitely
distracting, and sometimes it's
better actually to cook a meal,
go to a film, read a book, enjoy
visiting a new town, rather than
just reading about it online. Get
on with living your real life!

A–Z OF NETIQUETTE

A ☞ **ABBREVIATIONS** should only be used where appropriate and when you're sure the recipient will understand.
B ☞ **BREAK-UPS** should never be announced by text, email or via social network sites. C ☞ **CYBERBULLYING** it's easier to behave badly when you can hide behind the anonymity of the internet. D ☞ **DELETE** those friends who incessantly tag drunken photos you wouldn't want your boss, or your parents to see. E ☞ **EMOTICONS** can be interpreted as a childish substitute for proper self-expression. F ☞ **FRIEND REQUESTS** think carefully before accepting that 'friend' you met last night; do you really want them to know the ins and outs of your life?
G ☞ **GOBBLEDEGOOK** write clearly in the digital universe, and avoid jargon and acronyms. H ☞ **HEADPHONES** it's rude to use them when conducting everyday social transactions.
I ☞ **INAPPROPRIATE CONVERSATIONS** no stranger should have to listen to the intimate details of your relationship, health or finances. J ☞ **JAUNTY SIGN OFFS** don't end your business emails with a casual 'cheers' or 'see ya' – it's not appropriate for the context. K ☞ **KEEP SAFE** only give your home email address to colleagues and close friends and family.
L ☞ **LETTERS** – preferably handwritten – are a much better way of thanking someone for a present than texts.

M ☞ MISSED CALLS acknowledge them by calling back or sending a text. N ☞ NOMOPHOBIA are you suffering from a fear that your world will come to an end if you lose your mobile? O ☞ ONLINE DATING is full of potential for you to meet "The One". P ☞ PRIVACY should be a priority on the internet. Make sure you never reveal too much. Q ☞ QUIET ZONE have respect for your fellow passengers and don't use your phone in these areas. R ☞ RINGTONES say a lot about a person, ensure yours gives out the right message… S ☞ SPAMMING don't deluge your friends with endless links to websites, YouTube videos, and demands for signatures and sponsorship. T ☞ TABLE MANNERS the most important thing when sharing a meal with other people is to switch off your mobile and put it away. U ☞ UPDATING one's status incessantly will lead to some very bored and unhappy friends. V ☞ VOICEMAIL keep it short and sweet to ensure the person you are trying to reach will actually call you back. W ☞ WORKPLACE bitchy emails about a colleague are a risky business – email can be a very leaky medium. X ☞ XOXO are hugs and kisses really appropriate on messages to the boss? Y ☞ YAWN if all your conversation is based on information you've gleaned from the internet, people will suspect you of not having a life. Z ☞ ZZZZZ The End!

63

Also published by DEBRETT'S

Correct Form
Wedding Guide
Etiquette for Girls
Guide for the Modern Gentleman
Manners for Men
A-Z of Modern Manners
A Modern Royal Marriage
The Queen: the Diamond Jubilee

POCKET BOOKS:
Debrett's Men's Style

Debrett's also publishes an annual
range of stylish leather Lady's and
Gentleman's Diaries, with a wealth
of content that is designed to inspire,
inform and entertain.

Visit us at
www.debretts.com/shop